# *The* 5 STEP ACTION PLAN TO A HAPPY & HEALTHY *Marriage*

RABBI SHLOMO SLATKIN MS, LCPC

D1372182

# The 5 STEP ACTION PLAN TO A HAPPY & HEALTHY

## *Marriage*

INCREASE THE JOY OF SANCTITY,
SAFETY, AND STABILITY
IN YOUR HOME

Cover & Interior Design: KDG Advertising - www.kdga.net
Photo Credit: Istock Imaging
www.TheMarriageRestorationProject.com

1 With this ring . . . A national survey on marriage in
America. (2005). Gaithersburg, MD: The National Father-
hood Initiative

2 Stanley, S. M. (2005). The power of commitment: A guide to
active lifelong love. San Francisco:Jossey-Bass

3 Covey, Steven (1989). The Seven Habits of Highly Effective
People: Restoring the Character Ethic. Simon & Schuster Inc.

# AUTHOR'S BIO

Rabbi Shlomo Slatkin is a Licensed Clinical Professional Counselor, Certified Imago Relationship Therapist (Advanced Clinician), and an ordained Rabbi. He works with couples to empower them to develop a conscious and connected relationship through resolving conflict, learning communication skills, and rediscovering love. Rabbi Slatkin also uses this Imago couple therapy model with individuals, families, and organizations.

A gifted teacher who has lectured throughout the world, Rabbi Slatkin edited and co-authored the Jewish version of *Couplehood As a Spiritual Path*, a curriculum for synagogues based on Imago Relationship Therapy and Drs. Harville Hendrix and Helen LaKelly Hunt's *Getting The Love You Want*. He is also the author of *The Jewish Marriage Book: Improving Your Mar-*

*riage One Jewish Holiday at a Time*, as well as numerous published articles on relationships.

A graduate of Loyola University Maryland (formerly Loyola College), Rabbi Slatkin holds a master's degree in Counseling Psychology, with additional psychotherapy training at the Imago Relationship Institute. Rabbi Slatkin is a clinical member of the American Mental Health Counselors Association, Imago Relationships International, and the Mid-Atlantic Association of Imago Therapists.

# Table of Contents

# PREFACE

With the divorce rate reaching epidemic proportions, *The Marriage Restoration Project* was created to uphold the institution of marriage and family by providing proven resources that make a difference. Much like a piece of priceless art can be restored after years of neglect, so too a marriage has the potential to be restored to its original connection.

It is all too easy to discard an old relationship that no longer seems to function. We hold the hope for every couple to be able to experience profound growth and healingin their relationship. *The Marriage Restoration Project* aims to restore even the most stagnant of relationships by restoring and reawakening the original, undying connection that exists between you and your partner.

## INTRODUCTION

If you are reading this book, you are most likely experiencing marital crisis. Your life, as you know it, is under attack. You feel extremely unsafe and you don't know what to do. I have some good news for you. There is a way to protect yourself from the toxic energy that is destroying your relationship. In the following pages, you will learn a foolproof method for how to save your marriage, even if it is on the verge of destruction.

I remember about a year or so after 9/11 when there were warnings about the possibility of a chemical attack on the East Coast. My wife read up on how to protect us, ran to Home Depot, loaded up on supplies, and started sealing windows for a "safe room". We were terrified but felt a bit more capable of dealing with the threat after we took the necessary precautions. We learned that when dealing with any acute crisis, it is best to become informed and then decide what immediate action must be taken. We felt better having taken action.

The same applies to dealing with the crisis of your current relationship. You can point fingers and blame, you can come up with theories, and you can remain resentful, but if you do not take immediate action nothing will change and you'll continue to feel lousy.

## WHAT SHOULD YOU DO?

Take action. *The 5 Step Action Plan to a Happy & Healthy Marriage* will present you with a tried and true action plan, guiding you every step of the way. The Plan is based on my years of training in Imago Relationship Therapy and working with couples, as well as my own personal life experience.

## THE FIVE-STEPS ARE AS FOLLOWS:
## ACTION STEP I- COMMIT
## ACTION STEP II- SEAL YOUR EXITS
## ACTION STEP III- DETOX YOUR MARRIAGE
## ACTION STEP IV- ACKNOWLEDGE THE "OTHER"
## ACTION STEP V- LOVE INFUSIONS

In Steps I and II, you will learn how to make your marriage a priority, refocus, and bring the energy back into your relationship. Step III will teach you how to remove counterproductive behaviors such as negativity that seek to undermine your connection and then you will be able to create more safety in your relationship. In Step IV, you will learn how to acknowledge the "other," learning new ways to connect so that understanding each other and feeling respected and listened to becomes your marriage's second nature. Finally, Step V will teach you how to bring back some of the spark you once felt in your relationship.

As with any plan, this is a step-by-step process. This means that ideally you need to follow the sequence to reach your intended goal. There are a few ways to go about this:

*1) Read the book and stop to complete the exercises as you go along.*

*2) Read through the entire book one time without completing the exercises. Then read the book again, completing the exercises along the way.*

## Do I have to do the exercises?

Even if you choose option 2, you will inevitably have to do the exercises. The exercises are important because they will direct you in applying the material detailed in each action step to your personal situation. As you apply what you learn, you will bring about the desired change in your relationship. Otherwise, you will be reading about some interesting ideas that might stimulate your heart and your mind, inspiring you to see things differently, but in the end, you may lack the follow-through. The exercises will call you to act and therefore you can and will derive the maximum benefit from this book.

## HOW LONG WILL IT TAKE?

It really depends on the amount of work you are willing to put in. Some action steps may be easier to apply than others. Let's take, for example, Action Step V: Love Infusions. A love infusion such as an appreciation or a caring behavior can be applied immediately. On the other hand, Action Step III: Detox Your Marriage can take considerably longer depending on your motivation to watch what you say.

You may even find yourself working on all steps simultaneously. Although the steps have a logical progression, you can still benefit by detoxing your marriage (Action Step III) even if you are struggling with commitment issues (Action Step I). So even though it is best to go in order, don't refrain from applying all of the action steps to whatever degree you can, as they all can enable the others to be fulfilled harmoniously.

## WHO SHOULD READ THIS BOOK?

*The 5 Step Action Plan to a Happy & Healthy Marriage* can be implemented by couples or individuals. In my experience, there is usually one spouse that is less enthusiastic about working on the relationship. While working together with your spouse is optimal and will be especially helpful if you wish to work on the Imago Dialogue (to be detailed in Action Step IV), you can read this book and implement all of the Five Action Steps even if you have an unwilling spouse. All of the Action Steps can be done on your own and you can improve your relationship even without your spouse being directly involved. The reason for that is that this program is not about changing what's wrong with your spouse but about taking personal responsibility for your relationship. If you work on yourself, those changes have a ripple effect on your relationship and your spouse will change.

# Change yourself, change your relationship: a story

When you change the way you "show up" in your relationship, you may notice that your spouse's resistance begins to wane and many of your complaints about your spouse disappear. One of my favorite examples is the wife who would constantly ask her husband to do things for her. She was often faced with resistance. When she would ask him something, he would not provide a straight answer. He was full of excuses. As she started taking more responsibility around the house cooking dinner, doing the laundry, jobs that her husband previously did something interesting happened. Not only was he happier, he was much more responsive.

He no longer found himself threatened or annoyed by her requests because he knew that by taking on the role of the homemaker, she had taken action to give him more space. What changed? She changed, and not because of his complaints or because she felt she had to. She changed from a place of health and wellbeing. After certain events triggered her to take a look at why she'd been avoiding doing basic home-making tasks in the past, she became conscious about her feelings of resistance to being a home-maker. With that consciousness, she was able to make a decision that in the best interests of her family she needed to take more responsibility around the house. This change allowed her husband, always vigilant for fear of being taken advantage of, to relax.

The point of this story is that your relationship can improve by working on The Five-Step Action Plan, even without a willing spouse. Whether you read the book together with your spouse or go at it alone, I trust that you will find the The Five-Step Action Plan to be a user-friendly guide to achieving the relationship of your dreams!

## ACTION STEP I
## COMMIT

## COMMITTING TO THE RELATIONSHIP

Commitment issues are not only relevant to premarital couples. In fact, studies show that the number one reason for divorce is not money or infidelity, though they're up there, but lack of commitment.[1] While you may have committed to getting married, you were in love. It was easy! Although you may have been told that marriage has its ups and downs, you were too blind to see reality at the time. "No, we will be different, we won't fight, and we have a good relationship." Now, five, ten, twenty years down the road, you realize how right they were. You weren't prepared for this, and when you pledged to love each other "for better or for worse," you did not commit to something this "worse." This means that if you want to save your marriage, it is time to commit, but this time it is with the full knowledge of what that entails.

## What does it look like?

What does it mean to commit? Is it a decision, an attitude, an action? The good news is that if you are reading this book, it shows that you are already somewhat committed to your relationship; otherwise you wouldn't be interested in saving it. Commitment is a combination of all of the above. It requires a decision to be dedicated to the relationship, making it a priority in your life. That decision is followed by an attitude that your marriage comes first and you are willing to do what it takes to improve it. Finally, your actions for your marriage are the manifestation of your decision and your attitude. While the remaining Action Steps will focus on how to manifest your commitment in the world of action, Action Step One is making the decision to commit and developing an attitude of commitment.

## Why Should I commit?

The couples that successfully get through crisis are the ones who are committed to their marriage. In our disposable society, a marriage is as expendable as a computer. You buy it knowing that you will have to replace it within a few years. A marriage is not a computer. It is a serious commitment that requires work and while it may seem much easier to leave the relationship, the truth is that it won't necessarily be so. The potential damage divorce does will make you think twice about throwing away your marriage.

## TWO FORMS OF COMMITMENT

Let's examine some of the reasons why you should stay committed to your marriage. On a basic level, there are two forms of commitment- constraints and personal dedication.[2] Constraints are things that keep us in the relationship even if things are not going well. These include pressure from family and friends, financial concerns, children, negative beliefs about divorce, and fear of the future. While these constraints may be fear-based, they assist in keeping us from bolting when the going gets rough. However, these reasons are usually not enough in the long run.

What is needed for your relationship to endure is personal dedication, a real desire to be together with your spouse. It means making your relationship a priority and the willingness to sacrifice for the sake of the relationship. When this dedication is present, we feel safer and are more willing to give for the relationship to succeed. It helps us not get overwhelmed by the day-to-day challenges, as we have a long-term view of the marriage.

## DO IT FOR THE KIDS

If you are feeling lousy about your marriage, I imagine you may not necessarily feel like dedicating yourself to your relationship just yet. At the very least, though, you may have some constraints that may compel you to commit. The most compelling reason to think twice about calling it quits is your children. If you have a family, the damage that divorce can do to your children is exponential. Not only will it affect them when they get married but it will create pain and a host of mental health issues for them. Children of divorced parents are 50% more likely to get divorced themselves than children from unbroken homes. Divorce also doubles their risk of serious social, emotional, and psychological dysfunction. You may be unhappy in your marriage, but is it worth ruining the lives of your children as well?

While there is a common myth that your bad marriage, albeit intact, is worse for your kids in the long run, it just simply is not true. In spite of the fighting and unpleasantness, kids would much prefer to live in one world than have it split in two.

The collapse of the American family has destroyed our society. How many drug addicts, criminals, etc. grew up in a stable, two-parent household? Any guesses? When I worked in community mental health, I heard the saddest, most depressing stories of ruined lives that could have been so much better. Not one of those clients grew up in a two-parent household. When will we wake up and realize that many of our societal ills can be averted if we invest in fostering healthy relationships?

I cannot overemphasize the effect of an unstable home on your children. Many a time I will leave my office in the evening thinking about how so many of the couples I work with would not need my assistance if they did not have such traumatic childhoods. It is amazing the damage parents can do to their children. I see the effects on the next generation in their relationships and it is extremely upsetting. These are supposedly "normal" middle- to upper-middle-class families where the parents did not take ownership for their own emotional issues, which they probably inherited from their own parents. You have the unique opportunity to stop this "inheritance" and work on yourself so that you can provide a loving home that will nurture your children's emotional health. You may think divorce will solve the problem, but it won't. Take responsibility for your role in the marriage and work together with your spouse to create an environment where your children can thrive and develop into emotionally mature adults.

But what if I get remarried? Won't that provide my children with a stable home? Sorry to break it to you, but 65% of second marriages end in divorce. Second marriages with children are even more likely to be terminated. That means you run the risk of subjecting your children to another divorce. You are also making it more likely for your children to divorce later in life. Having a stepparent shows that spouses are expendable if they don't work out. Even if you stay married to your second spouse, there are still greater risk factors for children in stepfamilies.

## MONEY, MONEY, MONEY

If you are still not convinced or you don't have children, let's see what happens to your finances when you divorce. A newspaper headline recently stated that couples are refraining from divorce as it is too expensive. The high financial cost of divorce has been verified time and time again by various divorce attorneys with whom I have spoken. One attorney I know actually discourages couples from getting divorced. Besides lawyer fees, whatever remains is usually split in half. This means you will have less than half the amount of money you currently have. Where as money issues can cause marriage problems, terminating your marriage may only make it worse.

# No, You Won't Find Someone Better

As we see from the amount of divorces around us, these constraints were having less effect on keeping couples together. One major reason that you might be overlooking some of these realistic concerns is that you are convinced that your life could be better, especially if you are married to someone else. Maybe you married the wrong person. Despite the damage to your children and your finances, at least you could find someone else and live happily ever after. Well, I am sorry to burst your bubble, but this is a major fallacy. I have seen plenty of second marriages suffering from the same problems as were experienced in the first.

# "ARE YOU SURE I WON'T FIND SOMEONE BETTER?"

Part of being committed to your marriage, or at least trying to make it work, is to realize that it is not all about the other person. What do YOU bring to the table? Why is it possible to get divorced and have problems with a second marriage? Is it purely coincidence, bad luck? While you leave your ex behind, you take yourself into whatever relationship you join.

A relationship takes two to tango and there is never one party that is entirely innocent. What responsibility do we take for our relationship disaster? Is our spouse simply an evil monster with "psychological" problems or do we play a role in triggering such undesirable behavior? As we will learn a bit later, most of the things that really bother us about our partner are only partially about them and largely about us. Why would a particular incident bother you tremendously but appear insignificant to your friend?

Each one of us has our own unique history as well as natural tendencies. Both shape who we are and determine how we process events and/or react to others. Our external triggers, as real as they may be, are only a symptom of a greater problem. That problem is our story and ourselves. By working on ourselves and becoming more conscious about why we react the way we do, we can learn how to be more effective in our relationships and have more compassion for our spouse.

## Exercise Ia: Getting conscious about your triggers

Let's learn a little bit more about what bothers you so much about your spouse and why. Find a quiet place to sit down and either ponder or write down the answers to the following questions. If you have more than one annoyance, and you probably will, then you will want to answer the entire list of questions for each annoyance.

1) What annoys me about my spouse?

2) What hurts me so much about that?

3) What scares me about this?

4) How do I react?

5) What do I really need from my spouse?

6) What feels familiar about this experience?

****

Furthermore, these points of conflict are a blessing in disguise. Marriage is ultimately an opportunity for growth and healing. The challenges that we face are there to do just that, to challenge us to become better and more balanced people. The things that bother us most about our spouse or the things that our spouse complains about are usually the areas in which we could stand to experience more growth.

# A True Story

Do you remember the story in the beginning of the book about the wife that was domestically challenged? For years the husband had complained. He had wanted a wife who would be a stay-at-home mom. She ended up having a passion for working. Instead he became Mr. Mom. While he didn't mind cooking, he felt a bit emasculated and taken advantage of. In turn, he was so overwhelmed at home that he did not get his act together as a breadwinner. The wife, on the other hand, complained about his lack of motivation to grow his business and his general low self-esteem.

The things they disliked about each other were the very things each one of them needed to grow. Growing up in a divorced home with a feminist mom who pushed work over motherhood, the wife realized that she had judgments about staying home. Even though her mother always had dinner on the table, she was never encouraged to learn more about how to take control of a kitchen and turn it into a pleasurable experience. She didn't even know how to boil water! Accepting more responsibilities at home allowed her to look at parts of herself that she never wanted to look at before. Not only did it help her become more balanced, it gave her husband what he so desperately needed in a wife. In turn, that freed up the husband to concentrate on what he needed to do: be productive and make a living. Knowing that domestic chores would be taken care of, he could shift his focus elsewhere, feel better about himself, and curb his wife's anxiety about his livelihood.

If this conflict were not resolved, you may have suggested that they were wrong for each other. He should have married someone more motherly. In fact, on one of their dates she said she wasn't the "mommy type." He was too in love to really believe it, and he was in for a rude awakening. Yet his need, and subsequent frustration, was what compelled her to grow. And perhaps she should have married a professional with a good job. Her need for him to work was just what he needed for his own self-esteem, to be the breadwinner.

Thus your marriage crisis is not proof that you ended up with the wrong person; rather, it shows that you made the right choice. The hopes of someone better are futile because Mr./Mrs. Right will serve as a vehicle for your personal growth. After the honeymoon ends, your spouse will surely push your buttons, but still, this is not proof that you ended up with the wrong person. Might as well give it your all and make it work the first time instead of breaking up a family, spending lots of money on attorneys, and suffering additional heartache.

## RELATIONSHIP PEACE

What is more important than your marriage? If you don't have peace in your home then you will likely not have much peace of mind in anything you do. This reminds me of the following story:

There was once a Rabbi who stopped to rest at an inn. The innkeeper recognized who he was and asked for some private consultation time with the Rabbi. The innkeeper poured out his heart to the Rabbi. He complained about his wife and how she was so verbally abusive, giving him such a hard time about money and her overall nagging. While her husband was consulting with the Rabbi, the wife couldn't wait to put in her two cents. She couldn't wait to tell the Rabbi what was wrong with her husband. She piped up and told the Rabbi, "If there is no grinding in the mill, there is grinding in the home. If there is no business, there is no peace at home." The Rabbi replied, "On the contrary, if there is no grinding in the home, there is grinding in the mill. The best omen for business is peace in the home!"

*Would you not give all the money and time in the world for peace?*

## INVESTING IN YOUR RELATIONSHIP

Again, this means redirecting yourself to your spouse and committing to success instead of looking elsewhere for something or someone better. If divorce is always an option lurking in the back of your mind, you will not be able to be fully present in your relationship. You lack the commitment to make your relationship work. That is why a couple can come to counseling and still not succeed. Their commitment can be seen in their attitude and their actions. My successful couples are the ones who come consistently on a weekly basis. In the past, I had a sliding-fee scale based on joint gross income. Every once in a while I had couples complain about the fee, and in certain cases I lowered it. I can tell you that every couple that had a fee reduction was unsuccessful. In my judgment, they were not truly invested in their relationship. This not only showed in their success rate but in their attendance. They would cancel sessions, skip weeks, etc... It got to the point where I would make a fee reduction contingent on committing to 12 weekly sessions. I knew from experience that if they did not make such a commitment, they would not get the results they were looking for. An investment is not always pleasant but it is the best assurance that you will put in the necessary effort. Otherwise, you risk a loss.

My wife recently went to hear a talk given by a parenting expert. He has a host of programs available on CD, all rather costly. He explained to the audience that he charges so much because he wants the purchase to "hurt a bit." How many of you had bought self-help books or programs, only to have them sitting and collecting dust on your shelf? Unless you have unlimited finances, if you invested $500 in a set of CDs, you'd make sure you use them.

In my experience, couples in crisis that want their marriage to succeed and are willing to invest in their relationship are almost always successful. This holds true even for extramarital affairs. It is astonishing how, even with such a breach in the relationship, it is possible to salvage a marriage by committing to making it work. The ones who lack that commitment are the ones who don't always make it.

# The Freedom of Commitment

While you may be afraid of committing, once you decide to commit, you will actually feel much more relieved. A quote from a Starbucks cup: " The irony of commitment is that it's deeply liberating — in work, in play, in love. The acts frees you from the tyranny of your internal critic, from the fear that likes to dress itself up and parade around as rational hesitation. To commit is to remove your head as the barrier to your life."

It is often the case that indecision is what feels so uncomfortable and enslaving. Once we muster the courage to decide to commit, that stagnant energy can now move and propel you forward for the good.

The following are three written exercises to help you make the decision and develop the attitude of commitment.

# Exercise 1b - Committing to your marriage: Ask yourself the following questions

1) What is getting in the way of me committing to this relationship?

2) What is at risk for me to commit? What is so scary about it?

3) What will I gain if I do commit?

## Exercise 1c - Memory Lane

This is a fun exercise that you can even do together with your spouse. Oftentimes we forget why we fell in love. When we begin to think back on that wonderful time of courtship, we begin to remember that there was a good reason why we got married. This can provide us hope for our relationship.

Close your eyes and take a trip down memory lane, remembering the time when you first fell in love. As you remember that time, please share or write down three qualities that you found in your spouse that helped you know "he/she is the one for me." When you are done, explain or write down why those qualities were so important to you at that time.

## Exercise Id - Relationship Dream

In order to commit to the future of your relationship, it is essential to have a vision of how you see your relationship and where you see it going. Although it may appear to be just a dream, it is useful for providing you perspective, instead of getting stuck in some of the current difficulties you may be encountering. Take all the time you need to dream about where you see your relationship going. Do you hope you will grow old together and feel forever like best friends?

Do you wish to hold respect for each other even when times are difficult? When you are ready, write down a list of sentences that embody your dream. Remember to write in the positive and in present tense. Instead of "we do not fight,"write "we live peacefully together." Present tense is important because it brings your dream into the here and now, as if it is currently happening.

## Summary of Action Step I

Lack of commitment is the number one reason for divorce. In order to save your marriage you need to commit. Commitment is a decision, an attitude and an action. It is a decision to be dedicated to your relationship and place it as a priority. From this decision, you develop the attitude that your marriage comes first. Finally, your actions manifest that attitude.

It is important to commit because marriage is not expendable. It is not something that you just throw away when it is no longer working. There are also many potential problems you will face by getting divorced. If you have children, you will be splitting their world in two and putting them at great risk for divorce as well as psychological problems. You will also be worse off financially as you will have to split whatever remaining assets you have with your ex. Finally, you won't find someone better. As you have a role in your marital woes, you will also bring that same person, yourself, with you into any new relationship. Until you get conscious about your own triggers, you will likely experience similar marital unhappiness in your new relationship.

Marriage is for the purpose of growth and healing and your conflict with your spouse is actually proof you chose the right partner. In fact, conflict is a growth opportunity, compelling you to become a more complete person by changing the very areas that annoy your spouse but are also the most difficult for you to alter. Commitment enables you to achieve your own potential through your relationship.

Finally, there is nothing more important than relationship peace. It brings about all blessings. That is why it is crucial to truly be invested in your relationship. If you never make the decision to commit and you allow divorce to lurk in the back of your head as a constant option, you are not giving your marriage a fair chance.

# 5

## The

## ACTION STEP II
## SEAL YOUR EXITS

## SEAL YOUR EXITS

Now that you have committed to your relationship, it is time to get down to business. The first thing you need to do is to protect your marriage against external, negative influences that drain the energy from your relationship. It is time to create your very own "safe room," or safe space. That means sealing all energy leaks, window leaks, cracks in the wall — any possible exit coming from your home that could potentially be a hazard to yourself and your family, as well as shutting off any external air intake. Imagine your relationship as a sacred space in which any potential leakage or toxic intake could be fatal.

## Keeping the energy in your relationship

In order for a marriage to be a vibrant, living entity, energy must be present in the relationship. Before you can refocus yourselves on the energy between you and your spouse, you must make sure that no energy is leaking outside. An exit is an energy leak.

An exit is, essentially, any behavior you take when you don't know how to talk about your uncomfortable feelings with your spouse. These behaviors are conscious or unconscious ways to avoid dealing with each other. You either withdraw inside yourself or you go elsewhere looking to get your needs met. Whatever you choose, you will drain the relationship of its energy until it becomes lifeless. You, in effect, have filed for an "invisible divorce."

An "invisible divorce" means that you are basically roommates or business partners. While this is still better than actually getting divorced, it is a tragic way to live in a marriage. Many couples live like this until their children grow up and leave the house. At that point, they may feel there is no reason to continue living together. Becoming aware of your exits, sealing them, and learning how to revive your relationship can breathe fresh life into your marriage and make it thrive.

## Types of Exits

There are varying degrees of exits. Some are terminal, such as divorce, which permanently ends the relationship. Others are very serious, such as substance abuse or infidelity. The remaining exits are less severe but are so insidious and parasitical that they can do equal damage in the long run. These exits can be behaviors intentionally done to avoid your spouse, or even just behaviors you enjoy but which take energy and time away from your relationship.

While some of the latter are essential activities or valid forms of recreation, if one of the reasons you are doing this activity is to avoid spending time with your spouse, it is considered an exit.

### *Here is a list of fourteen common exits that I imagine many of us do:*

| | |
|---|---|
| Work | Overeating |
| Exercise | Internet/Email |
| Entertainment/TV | Housework |
| Hobbies | Taking care of the kids |
| Sleeping | Talking on the phone w/ frie |
| Avoiding eye contact | Reading |
| Affair | Emotional Infidelity |

There are surely other exits that do not appear on this list. Whatever your exits are, it is important to recognize them and understand that these are forms of "acting out" your frustrations about your marriage. Just as our children may "act out" when they are hungry or not getting enough attention, adults react similarly when their needs are not being met. Instead of having a tantrum, we escape the marriage.

## GETTING YOUR NEEDS MET ELSEWHERE

When you feel unloved, ignored, or unappreciated, you go everywhere but to your spouse to get those needs met. You find others and/or other activities that will meet those needs or you withdraw within yourself, feeling hopeless about ever getting what you want. It is understandable why these exits could be problematic for your relationship. First of all, they can be very time-consuming, taking away possible time you could invest in your relationship. Even more danger-ous is the possibility of developing an emotional connection with a member of the opposite sex, as will be explained, which often leads to a slippery slope of activities that will devastate your mar-riage. Finally, you may feel so satisfied by getting your needs met elsewhere that you will lack the motivation needed to work on your relationship.

Yet at the same time, it makes sense why you would exit your relationship when the go-ing gets tough. We are mandated by our call to survive to get our needs met. When they are not met, we become angry or afraid and avoid inti-macy. Without the proper communication skills, it is often too threatening to share our frustra-tions about these unmet needs with our spouse. It is a lot safer to call a friend and complain about your husband or to do the dishes when you are upset with your wife. In the long run, though, it is much better for the relationship when we keep the energy that belongs in the relationship where it needs to be and not drive it elsewhere.

Sometimes, you may find exits enjoyable. That's understandable. After all, why would you want to talk to your spouse when it often ends in a screaming match, when you could go on Facebook, and have a funny, pleasant, pleasurable conversation with a friend? But if you want to save your marriage, don't take that exit, even if it is more pleasurable.

If you find the exit more enjoyable than where your marriage is right now, I'd encourage you to revisit the memory lane exercise and remember when you first fell in love. Try to hold onto that visual, even if it seems so distant. Open your wedding album if you have to, or go back to your dating picture album and TRUST that your marriage can become even more exciting and enjoyable than an exit.

# The Ultimate Destroyer

In transforming your relationship into a "safe room," it is important to examine all of the energy leaks that may be present in your relationship. Many of the exits listed above, alone, do not destroy a marriage; rather they contribute to the "invisible divorce."

If you are in crisis, there is something that has pushed you over the edge. Here is what I have found to be the death knell to even the lousiest marriages... infidelity. I am not just talking about extramarital affairs, but any activity in which you are disloyal to your spouse. Couples in crisis are often facing everywhere but towards each other and their relationship. They are caught up in the sea around them, their friends, their family, and/or their therapists.

*Here are some stories I have heard from more than one couple:*

"We've been married twenty years and it has been pretty bad, but now I have no desire to work on the relationship and I am ready for divorce."

What happened? Years of bad marriage counseling that didn't help, yet they still stayed together? What was the straw that broke the camel's back? I had a pretty good guess before they even told me. When did things take a turn for the worse?

"A few years ago I started seeing an individual therapist ..." The wife was told by her therapist that it was better to work with her privately and "fix" her own problems than to work together with the husband. The therapist would even ask the husband what he would like his wife to work on. Let's just say it was a disaster.

She became so attached to the therapist that she had "worked on herself" and concluded that her husband was the problem. She was done and there was no way I could even invite her to do couples work with him.

Or what about the therapist who convinced a wife to leave her husband without even inviting him to join a therapy session and meet him!

Or the manipulative know-it-all male friend who was planting seeds into the wife's head that her husband was no good? A few years back she "counseled" her male friend and tried to save his disastrous marriage. Now he, a divorced man, is giving marriage advice?

I almost always know that there is "infidelity" (whether an actual affair or an energy leak) happening when there is absolutely no interest in working on the relationship. I often am prompted to ask in such a case if there is an affair. If there isn't, there is usually a therapist or another "advice-giver" involved. I can always hear when there is the voice or influence of another. It is particularly sad because the relationship is usually salvageable.

This is the danger of airing your dirty laundry in public. No one is neutral. If your confidants are friends or family, they will be more concerned about your own well-being than your relationship's well-being. Your confidants may also have a personal axe to grind with your spouse or even have their own agendas, as in the case of the male "friend" above.

"But what could possibly be wrong with a therapist?" you may ask. While individual therapy is often helpful for individuals, it is often counterproductive for couples going through marital problems. Individual therapy can be so dangerous for your marriage because it shifts the energy away from your relationship — the true healing vehicle for your marriage. Both you and your spouse have all the answers you need to repair your relationship. It is not helpful when a therapist speaks poorly about your spouse or gives you advice that you can't contain when you get home, so you feel as if you must start "criticizing" your husband or wife. It leads to insecurity and second-guessing. If you come home disagreeing with your spouse, saying, "Well, my therapist said," then you may want to become a little more aware of the influence your individual therapy is having on your marriage.

Even the most well-meaning individual therapists can be harmful if they are advising you about your spouse when he/she isn't there. If you are seeing an individual therapist for your marriage, the best thing you can do is work on your issues alone and ask the therapist not to make any suggestions about your spouse.

Unless there is physical abuse or potential threat to one's life, it is irresponsible for a therapist to encourage divorce without hearing both sides of the story. Ultimately, it is the couple's decision.

The moral of all these stories: If you are in crisis, cut out the peanut gallery. Although they may be well meaning, they will often do more harm than good for your relationship, as their main concern is you (if you're lucky) and not your relationship.

A brief qualification: I do not believe all individual therapy is harmful for a marriage, nor do I believe that it is the primary cause for bad marriages or divorce. Bad marriages lead to divorce and the main culprit is the couple. Unfortunately, there are many therapists who supply input in a way that does more damage than good. Just as with any profession, not all therapists are competent or have competency in dealing with the delicate issues that a couple in crisis presents. It is all too easy to hear one side of the story, draw conclusions, and provide advice. Therapists or any other third party must be careful not to get "sucked in." Rather, they must listen with compassion and help the individual understand his or her own feelings about the situation without passing judgment on the spouse that is not present.

While it would be ideal for all couples in crisis to get help as a couple, it does not always work that way. Many individuals are crying out in pain and need someone to talk to and help them work out their issues. If their spouse is not willing to get help together, they may feel that their only option is individual therapy. Individual therapy can be helpful in such a situation and help the individual return to the relationship stronger. However, it is important for the consumer to be aware of the aforementioned issues as they are common enough to warrant a warning.

## An Affair

But what if you or your spouse actually had an extramarital affair? According to the *Journal of Couple and Relationship Therapy*, approximately 50 percent of married women and 60 percent of married men will have an extramarital affair at some time in their marriage. An affair is probably the most devastating blow you can give to your relationship. It completely destroys any remnant of trust you may have had with your spouse as well as the sanctity of your marital union. After we work on the affair and close all exits, we then spend time working on the relationship and exploring what was not previously working that led to such a serious breach.

Just as we have observed with other couples in crisis, the most successful couples battling an affair are those who sealed their relationship room. I had one couple who told their social circle that they were taking a break to work on their relationship and would not be hanging out with them for a while. This is what they needed to do to keep the energy where it needed to be.

It goes without saying that the affair must be stopped and all contact with that person must cease. Without this, it is almost impossible to work on the relationship. If your spouse is madly in love with someone else, they are chemically connected to that person and will be unwilling and even unable to repair your marriage. Resolving to end the affair is a prerequisite to reintroducing safety into your relationship.

Another precaution that must be taken is that you should not put yourself in a test by placing yourself back in the same situation in which you experienced the affair. Don't visit the same haunts where you met this person. Avoid other venues where you may be tempted to connect with members of the opposite gender. Besides social settings, this also means Internet chat rooms and social networking websites. I just heard of a study that found that 20% of divorce papers mentioned Facebook as a factor in divorce. There is so much out there and so many temptations and opportunities to throw your marriage away for a fleeting pleasure. Any avenue that you fear may lead you on such a path must be closed. While, in general, the middle path is the way to go, when one does something so extreme, one must temporarily take the opposite extreme to get back to the middle.

Even when there is no actual affair involving physical contact but an emotional connection with a member of the opposite sex, it does tremendous damage to the relationship. In our society, it is commonplace to double-date or to have both male and female friends. After working with countless numbers of couples, it is my opinion that this is "playing with fire." It is not very hard to cross the line between friend and love interest. If you are experiencing stress in your marriage and feel ignored by your spouse, it may take just a little attention from another man or woman to make you feel better. That attention very easily turns into emotional and physical intimacy. You may think you are strong or moral person and would never be subject to temptation, but what you are taking is basically a calculated risk.

Furthermore, socializing with other couples may also bring up doubts for you about your spouse. If you are suffering, the grass is always greener on the other side, "If I were only married to him/her, I would be happy." While these feelings often stem from insecurity and relational immaturity, it is still another opportunity to sabotage your relationship.

If you want to save your marriage, you must create that safe "relationship room" so that you can shut off negative outside influences and keep the energy where it belongs. From the most benign conflict to an extramarital affair, this must be your priority. Only then can you begin to experience healing and repair.

The sealing process is like to facing everywhere but each other, back to back, then turning around and facing each other. It literally enables your relationship to do a 180. What do I mean? You are face to face. What do you see? When I work with couples, I have them face each other. The comments I get range from "You want me to look at him?" to "We haven't faced each other in years!"

Often couples comment that the shift in dynamic, from facing everywhere but each other to facing each other, leaves a tremendous impact and provides hope for the relationship. Instead of talking about each other, they are talking to each other. They are face to face with the one they fell in love with. I believe that their connection is still there but it is buried deep underground as years of pain have concealed it. Facing each other, both figuratively and literally, is the beginning of the process of healing. You have eliminated outside forces sucking the energy from your relationship. Now you are ready to begin the work of repair.

## Exercise IIa: How to Seal Your Exits

Let's begin the process of closing your exits. This is a great way to become more aware of the behaviors that you engage in to avoid being in the relationship, and it may motivate you to start putting more energy back into your marriage.

1. Make a list of your exits. How do you escape your marriage? Through work, friends?

2. Place a check by those exits that are easy for you to change and an "x" by those that are difficult to change.

3. Then pick one of the exits that are difficult for you to change, such as staying late at work, and complete the following sentences:

a) The feeling I am avoiding by doing this activity is...

b) When I take this exit, how it affects my relationship is ...

c) And if in the future I continue to take this exit, what I expect to have in my relationship is ...

d) One thing I could do differently than take this exit is...

e) And if I tried to do this new behavior I would probably feel...

Use this process for all of your exits and then gradually begin closing them. This may mean picking one exit a week to work on. For others it could take less time, and others more time.

## Exercise IIb- identifying your peanut gallery

1) Who do you instinctually call when something goes wrong? If it's not your spouse, who is it, and why is he or she the first one you call?

2) Start noticing what you say about your spouse. Who do you talk to about your spouse?

3) Is your therapist feeding you ideas about your spouse?

4) Are people familiar with every intimate detail of your marriage?

## Summary of Action Step II

An exit is a way of escaping your marriage when the going gets tough. It is necessary to seal your exits, protecting against external negative influences that drain energy from your relationship. Some exits may be seen as benign activities such as watching TV, yet if they are done to avoid the relationship, then they must be altered.

When couples exit their marriages, they get their needs met elsewhere. This can be dangerous for the relationship as it could lead to terminating the relationship.

One of the most damaging exits is "infidelity." This is any action that demonstrates disloyalty to the relationship. Those who commit "infidelity" are no longer interested in the relationship. While an extramarital affair is an extreme version of infidelity, individual therapy, family, and friends are all avenues through which we air our dirty laundry, and through which we can be influenced negatively. It is important to be aware of what information we are getting fed by others and if it negatively affects our relationship with our spouse.

Extramarital affairs require specific vigilance regarding exits that led up to the affair, including relationships with members of the opposite sex, socializing with couples, etc. By not being tempted by those same exits, we refocus the energy where it belongs: our marriage.

In order to be able to repair your relationship and bring in new energy, it is essential to close all exits that are draining your marriage.

# ACTION STEP III: DETOX YOUR MARRIAGE

Now that you have decided that you want your marriage to work, remove the negativity. If you are in a sealed room filled with poison, your odds of survival are not too good. Removing the negativity allows you to take all of the poison out of your relationship.

This can be very hard because you've been hurt. How can you not harp on past wrongdoings? Yet to move forward, you must eliminate blame, shame, and criticism to the best of your ability. Otherwise, all of the "relationship vitamins" you may be taking will not be very effective unless you first flush out the toxins.

# Verbal Abuse

Abuse in any relationship is unacceptable. While society has thankfully condemned domestic violence, whose main perpetrator is men, female verbal abuse has gotten a pass. Men's strength is physical while women's strength is verbal. It is as if it is socially acceptable for women to bully their husbands. Just as one should not hit use fists to express relationship frustration, one should not lash out with their tongue to voice relationship grievances. There are safer and more effective ways to communicate such feelings, as we will learn later on. Verbal abuse slowly chips away at the trust present in a relationship and often leaves it hard to rebuild.

In the book *How to Improve Your Marriage Without Talking About It*, Drs. Patricia Love and Steven Stosny explain that couples disconnect due to fear and shame. For example, men and women fear homelessness equally, though in different ways. If you were to ask a woman what she would be most afraid of if she became homeless, her main fears would be bodily harm, isolation, and deprivation. Most men would say that the most difficult part of becoming homeless would be feeling like a failure. While safety may be an issue for men, the utter shame of being on the street and unemployed is their primary concern. When women shame their husbands by nagging them to make more money, go on more job interviews, and complain they don't do anything, often because they themselves may be experiencing fear, they are touching a particularly sensitive spot. The results can be devastating to a man. He is going to have a hard time if he feels he is being accused or criticized and will feel even more disconnected from her.

This does not exempt the husband from his responsibility to provide for his wife and allay her fears. Of course, he must do his due diligence to earn a livelihood. At the same time it is important for women to realize the effect their "encouragement" may have on their husbands. Criticism and unsolicited advice can feel unsafe and produce the opposite of the desired result. Learning how to express your fears in a safe, non-confrontational manner is the best way to be heard and to achieve your goal.

## FINDING THE REQUEST UNDERNEATH THE FRUSTRATION

As you begin to eliminate the negativity, ask yourself, "What do I want?" Underneath every frustration we experience lies a request or an unmet need. What do you need from your spouse? My children were fighting the other day and my wife stopped them and said, "Stop fighting and ask for what you want." The bottom line is that you are angry because there is something from your spouse that you are not getting. Asking directly for what you want is a much more productive way to get what you need. Nagging, blaming, shaming, or criticizing goes does nothing except to drive the other person away.

## ASK FOR WHAT YOU WANT

There is an important rule to asking for what you want. Be careful NOT to add a threat to your request. For instance, if you ask your spouse to spend more time with you and you add that you will go elsewhere if the request is not met, you are unlikely to get the results you truly want as you are setting up an unsafe environment. The main thing is to be able to ask for what you want in the context of safety.

# The Problem with Negativity

Detoxing your marriage means ridding your relationship of negativity. This may seem like a daunting task, yet it is crucial for the health of your relationship. The more negative experiences we have with our spouse, the more we become conditioned to view him or her in a negative light. We reinforce those negative neural pathways in our brain, causing us to get further stuck in our negativity. The good news is that our brains have neuroplasticity, which means they can change. New neural pathways can be formed and we can learn to experience each other in a different, more positive way. It may take time to change old habits that have been reinforced over time, yet by detoxing your relationship and practicing love infusions, as you will learn later on in Action Step 5, you will be on your way to remolding your experience with your spouse to something positive.

# ANGER - A MOST DESTRUCTIVE FORCE

One of the most dangerous manifestations of negativity in a relationship is anger. Most of us get upset with our spouses at times and many of us may express our feelings with strong emotion. When we convey those feelings with anger or rage, it has a devastating effect both on our partner and on ourselves. While it may feel like a relief to get out your frustration, you leave your spouse feeling more hurt and disconnected. Although you may regret what you did after the fact, anger can leave permanent scars on the heart of your loved one.

Anger is powerful and can be extremely scary. When we are angry, we are often no longer "in control" of ourselves. This is a frightening sight to experience and even if you feel that your spouse, who is the recipient of your explosion, is in the wrong, there are other, more effective ways to get across your message.

# How do I stop?

While Action Step 4 will provide more insight into how to be in your relationship in a safe way, Action Step 3 calls on you to eliminate the negativity and lashing out. This does not mean to suppress your feelings, of course, as that may do more damage in the long run. What it does mean is taking responsibility for your feelings and speaking about them in a mature way.

One way to accomplish this is by making "I" statements. Instead of criticizing, blaming, or shaming when we are feeling hurt, try: "I feel sad or belittled when you talk to me like that." When you put the focus on yourself, you are decreasing the potential for reactivity from your spouse. While one can dispute the facts, one cannot argue about a feeling. By making an "I" statement, you have removed the threat, and in turn, created safety.

## You have the power to change

One of the most empowering aspects of Action Step 3 is that you alone can shift the energy of your relationship by detoxing your marriage. Even if your spouse is not willing to work on the relationship, the effort that you make in eliminating blame, shame, negativity, and anger will have a huge impact. As you remove the toxicity that you bring into the relationship, your spouse will begin to be more open to experiencing a new you, and in turn, respond accordingly. A toxic relationship is a vicious cycle where spouses feed off of each other. Once one spouse stops the cycle on his or her end, there will often be no need for the other to continue spewing negativity, as it is usually a reactive response in the first place.

# Exercise IIIA-
# Transforming frustration

While similar to exercise IA, Getting Conscious About Your Triggers, this exercise takes it a step further by helping you discover a new way to articulate your frustrations.

1) List all of your frustrations with your spouse.

2) Write down how you would normally articulate them to your spouse.

3) Do I express these frustrations from a place of shame, blame, or criticism? If so, what is it that I really want from my spouse, and how could I articulate it in a more healthy and effective way?

## Summary of Action Step III

Now that you have sealed the energy leaks, it is time to detox the negative energy that remains. This means removing the poison from your relationship by eliminating all blame, shame, and criticism.

Verbal abuse is a no-no and can be devastating to a relationship, especially for men. Remember that the more men feel shamed, the more incapable they become, and the more fear that will evoke for women. Nip it in the bud by speaking respectfully.

When you feel frustrated, think of the request that lies beneath the surface. Stop fighting and ask for what you want. Your spouse cannot read your mind so asking directly is the most effective way of getting your needs met. While you ask, make sure you don't threaten, as that would be counterproductive.

You can stop the negativity by taking ownership for your feelings in the form of "I" statements. Also, think about your triggers and how you could express yourself in a more effective manner.

# Action Step IV: Acknowledge the "Other"

In Action Step I, you committed to being in your relationship. In Action Step II, you removed outside influences and closed exits that were distracting you from being in your relationship. In Action Step III, you purged the actual negativity from your relationship. You are now ready to acknowledge the "other." This means being in your relationship in an entirely new way, by learning how to listen and talk with your spouse in a manner that brings about greater connection and less reactivity.

You can acknowledge the other both when you speak and when you listen. If you are the speaker, you will first consider what your goal is for bringing up the topic of discussion and whether it is a good time for your spouse to listen. If you are the listener, you will want to prepare yourself to realize that this is not about you, but about the "other," even if you know you are about to be criticized.

## Keep the Goal in Mind

The first step to acknowledging the other is keeping the goal in mind. This means that when you engage in your relationship, you have a clear intention of what you want to accomplish. Do you want to connect or disconnect? When you speak to your spouse, what are the desired results? As you examine the intended results, think about how you can achieve those results. Is yelling at your spouse going to bring you closer together? Probably not, so it is important to act in a way that helps you achieve your goal of connection.

If you have decided that your goal is to connect, then you must create a safe environment in which to share. This is accomplished by first making sure it is a good time to talk. Did you ever walk in the door hungry and tired from a long day of work, only to be greeted by your spouse's grievances? Or maybe you were in the middle of writing an important email and your spouse interrupted you to talk about an issue? If you catch your spouse off-guard, you are not giving him or her a chance to show up with his or her best, attentive, and loving self.

If you want your spouse to listen and hear your story and not be reactive, you MUST make sure it is a good time to talk. In the case of a husband coming home from work wanting to complain to his wife about the house being in disarray, he would be setting her up for fight/ flight mode by spontaneously "dumping," expecting her to listen intently without responding. She will not appreciate being told what she did wrong or how much she frustrates him if she has not been asked if now is a good time to talk.

"Dumping" is threatening and will prevent your spouse from feeling safe enough to listen and there for you. Ask yourself, "What is my intention for having this conversation?" Do you, want your spouse to really hear you or do you just wish to hurt or dump on him or her? The intention of any interchange, no matter how challenging the issue, must be connection.

So what do you do when you need to talk about something difficult with your spouse? You ask him/her, "I would like to make an appointment to share something with you. Is now a good time?" I even have couples in their sessions make an appointment with each other (while they're sitting there) to talk about an important issue, even though the entire reason they showed up for the session was to do this work! Nevertheless, it trains them to show concern for the listener on the receiving end. It opens the receiver up to being available to enter the world of the other. When the person listening has advance notice, he/she is more likely to hear you in a less defensive way.

## TAKING A RAIN CHECK

What happens if now is not a good time? This is often actually a good thing. There is usually one spouse who is more impulsive and ready to unleash at a moment's notice. If your spouse is unable to listen at this time, it will provide a chance for the intensity to abate. Once it is no longer as urgent, you can express the frustration in a more conscious and less reactive way. This is also beneficial for the listener because if now is not a good time — having just gotten home from work and hungry, or being mentally and emotionally not able to listen — he/she will not be set up for an escalation of tension.

There is one caveat here. If a request for an appointment cannot be met immediately, it should be rescheduled, preferably within the next 24 hours, or as soon as possible thereafter. If one spouse constantly says it is not a good time, the spouse who wants to talk will never have the chance to express his/her feelings and will feel unheard and resentful. An appropriate response would be, "Now is not a good time and I really want to hear what you have to say. Could we talk later tonight when I get home?" Scheduling within the next 24 hours shows that you are not pushing your spouse off, and even though you may not really want to hear what your spouse has to say, you are giving him/her a time when you will be more available and feel safer. Once the appointment is made it shows the sender that you care and some of the steam will subside.

## WHAT IF YOUR SPOUSE ISN'T READING THIS BOOK

If your spouse isn't reading this book, he/she may not know about making an appointment and creating safety. Nevertheless, you can still have your goal of connection in mind when you initiate a discussion by asking if it is a good time to share. This will make your spouse feel safer, and in turn, help him/her feel more comfortable to engage fully in the relationship. After awhile, he/she may even catch on.

You, the reader, are also about to learn how to listen in a way that acknowledges the "other" and leaves you protected. Follow the recommendations for the listener.

# ENTERING THE WORLD OF THE OTHER

The second step to acknowledging the other is to enter his or her world. What this means is to really be able to listen to another person and understand him or her in the context of his or her reality, not your own. The number one reason people are not able to really listen to their spouses is their inability to enter the other's world and validate his or her experience. Ego and self-absorption prevent us from making this "trip." We're worried it means giving up our own opinions or losing ourselves if we fully listen.

This does not mean that you must be a doormat and let others walk all over you; it means being able to make space for the other in relationship. This is difficult because we tend to see things through the vantage point of the self. In fact, a degree of self-absorption is necessary for our survival. If we had no self-interest, we would not eat, protect ourselves from danger, etc. However, in our effort to remain safe, we create our own little world. In this world, we assume that everyone experiences life as we do and we have a hard time making sense of anything else.

Have you ever had a food that you especially enjoyed? Now imagine you encountered someone who found it terribly unappealing, even nauseating. In Imago Relationship Therapy, this is an example of what we call "symbiosis." Since we wouldn't eat it, no one else would, either. Can you imagine if you met someone who didn't like ice cream? "How could you not like ice cream?!" The list goes on an on, from your favorite music, to your doctor, to your political party, etc. We believe that if we like something or think a certain way, then everyone else must agree.

While preferences are by nature subjective, what about our own, individual truth/experience about an objective incident? This symbiosis stretches to the point that we are unable to make sense of the experience of the other because it differs from ours. Not only does it not make sense, but we begin to feel unsafe, especially when it focuses on something we may have done. We, in turn, respond from a place of fear, and that drive to stay alive that protected us so nicely is now destroying our family life. We become reactive and we can't even listen.

To break our natural reactivity, we need to create an almost artificial process to retrain our brain. One of the goals of acknowledging the other is to break this symbiosis, to take the "I" out of the listener so that we can truly hear what our spouse is saying. The structure of making an appointment and keeping the goal in mind makes it safe for the listener so that he/she will not revert to his/her defenses. It slows down the process so that we can be intentional about what we say and really listen to what is being said. Not only will you be able to understand your spouse better and not react and create further discord, your spouse will feel understood.

## LEARNING HOW TO LISTEN

Even if we don't become defensive or confrontational, we have a few things to learn about listening. Suppose a husband had a major presentation tomorrow at work and he shared his feelings of anxiety with his wife. Here are a few typical, benign, non-reactive responses that may occur:

| Commiserating | Unsolicited Advice | Discounting Feelings |
|---|---|---|
| Oh, I see. I hear you. | You could do some breathing exercises before you speak. You should take some medication if you are feeling so anxious. | You shouldn't be nervous. Don't worry about it. There is nothing to worry about. |
| I know what it's like. I also get nervous when I have to speak in front of a large audience. | | You'll do a great job. |

While all of these responses are well in-tentioned, giving unsolicited advice, discounting feelings, and commiserating will often leave the person feeling unsatisfied and unheard. The reason they do not work is that they are focused more on the listener, perhaps from a place of anxiety, than on the one talking. True listening is other-centered.

When fully in the other person's world, the listener does not interject her own opinions. She must be completely focused on the other, so much so that she cannot even lend words of encouragement. Her sole task is to make sure she really understood what her husband said. This is especially effective when dealing with touchy subjects that may provoke a reaction on her part. Instead of getting into her "stuff," her reactivity stemming from his experience, she is forced to leave her world behind temporarily and journey into the world of her husband. Perhaps she thinks he is completely wrong, makes absolutely no sense, and does not have the facts straight. It doesn't matter. It is not about right or wrong. As the saying goes, "You can be right or you can be in a relationship." It is possible that both are correct in their own eyes.

Accept that you are in a relationship with an "other" and that "other" has his or her own experiences, a unique way of viewing the situation, and a right to their own opinion.

Furthermore, it is not really about the particular issue or grievance being addressed, but about something deeper. In the case of the husband coming home and expressing anger at the messy house, if she develops curiosity for his story, she may discover what is really bothering him. Not only will she feel relieved that it really wasn't all about her and how horrible she is, she may feel compassion for his story — for example, seeing him as a little boy who often came home to a messy house due to very volatile family relations. This is the magic of the 90/10 rule. The 90/10 rule dictates that 90% of anything that intensely bothers us is due to the triggering of a past experience or feeling and 10% of our reaction is due to the particular stimulus at hand.

The strong emotions that this husband felt are merely old feelings reawakened by this incident. While this does not absolve him from responsibility to speak respectfully, if you were the wife, it would have been helpful to have this rule in mind to prevent you from being reactive when confronted with his barrage of emotions or criticism.

Anytime a moment of contention occurs, remind yourself that your spouse is not picking on you, but that he or she is in pain and it is time for you to get a little curious about his or her story.

Thus, learning how to listen helps us realize that our spouse's frustration is ultimately not about us. When we come to such a realization, we feel less threatened by their grievances and can become more receptive to them and their needs, thus eliminating much needless conflict, stemming from misunderstanding and reactivity.

## Taking your listening to the next level

If what I have said so far resonates with you and you want to follow a formula that all of my successful couples practice, you are ready to learn about the Imago Couple's Dialogue. The dialogue creates an almost artificial new way of being in a relationship, a new way of talking. The dialogue process is very structured, and although it may feel a little uncomfortable at first, it works wonders. Couples love the results it produces as it allows them to talk without fear of interruption or retaliation. It also slows things down and allows both to feel heard. After just one session, couples explain that they have not had such a conversation in years, if ever. While all of their problems will not be solved after one time, they leave with a hope of being able to learn a new skill, a skill that will teach them how to be in their relationship in a whole new way.

We really do want to be in a relationship but we are scared. Unless we can create safety and learn how to trust one another again, we will not feel safe enough to engage in a relationship. This lack of safety manifests itself as not talking, not opening up, or attacking the other to get attention.

Lack of safety is why traditional marriage counseling is often so ineffective. What husband wants to pay money to hear himself get blamed and shamed by his wife in front of a stranger? What wife wants to pay to be told it is her problem, that she is wrong, and here are the changes she must make? That model only contributes to further discord. Creating an atmosphere of safety makes seeking assistance much more inviting.

## How does the dialogue work?

In a dialogue, there is a sender (the one talking) and a receiver (the one listening). The dialogue process allows the sender to feel truly heard. This is accomplished by having the receiver mirror what the sender says. The receiver simply repeats or paraphrases what their spouse says and then asks if he or she got it, and if there is more the sender wants to share. This continues until the sender says everything he or she want to express.

While my couples often first remark that this is not a "normal" way of talking, mirroring does wonders for relationships.

## THE DIALOGUE - AN EXAMPLE

Here is a real example of a situation that went right with dialogue and could have easily turned into a fight without it:

*Wife:* I am really upset that you haven't gone to the cleaners to get your shirts cleaned. I feel like I have to do everything for you ... like you are one of the kids, another person to take care of. If I don't take care of it, nobody will.

He actually disagrees with his wife. The husband was fully intending to go to the cleaners. In fact, he was scheduled to go today. He also does a lot to help around the house and he had never asked his wife to go to the cleaners! His natural reaction would be to politely dissent and tell his wife "the truth" and clear his name. If he made that choice, an argument most likely would have ensued and it would have resulted in rupture. Fortunately, this husband had learned the dialogue and he took the risk of not being right in order to enter the world of his wife. Here was his real response:

*Husband: So what I heard you say* is that you are upset that I did not go to the cleaners and get my shirts cleaned and that you feel like you have to do everything for me, as if I am one of the kids. *Did I get you? (Meaning, did I understand what you said?)*

*Wife:* Yes.

*Husband: Is there more?* (Meaning, is there more you want to share with me, because I am interested in hearing your story.)

The dialogue continued until the wife realized that this reminded her of how she once felt pressured to take care of her siblings, because her parents were not always available. This situation with the dry cleaners triggered that anxiety she experienced as a little girl. When she was finished sharing the story, her husband had fully made the journey into his wife's world. He realized that it had very little to do with him or right or wrong. He was able to have compassion for his wife, for the little girl who was forced to grow up too soon. His eyes even filled with tears. He concluded the dialogue by validating her feelings.

**Husband: *What you are saying makes sense*** because I didn't go to the cleaners. (Even though he may have intended to go later that day, and never asked his wife, he admitted his 10%.)

Finally, he empathized by sharing with his wife how he imagined she might be feeling.

*Husband: I imagine you may be feeling* very overwhelmed and alone. *Is that what you're feeling?*

As a result of the dialogue, a shift occurred. When the husband was able to journey into his wife's world, not reacting to or contending the facts, she was able to feel heard, and instead of resulting in disconnect, their exchange brought them closer than they had been in months!

When leading couples through dialogue, I often give them the image of crossing over a bridge into the world of the other. When we are able to view our spouse as other than ourselves, someone with different experiences, views, and opinions, we are much more able to make sense of their feelings and behavior. Have you ever visited another culture? While you may have felt a bit uneasy, did you ever feel your way of life to be threatened? Were you able to respect the way they do things even if you did not agree with their lifestyle? It is much easier to be respectful of a lifestyle that does not encroach upon yours. It is only when you get close to home that you feel threatened. When we realize that our spouse is not us, we can then enter their world without feeling threatened. We can play by their rules and follow the local custom because we are just visiting. And don't worry; it is not a one-way trip. Your spouse will have plenty of opportunities to visit your world and experience your different perception of reality, all in the spirit of goodwill and connection. After a while, you will begin to accumulate a lot of frequent flier mileage and your life will be enriched by your travels.

# What to do if your spouse isn't reading this book

If your spouse isn't reading this book, you can still start your own healing process by mirroring your spouse. Your spouse will begin to feel validated and heard, leading to less reactivity and discord. Make it natural, paraphrasing if you have to, rather than sounding robotic.

Mirroring protects you because it forces you to respond in an intentional way, as opposed to a knee-jerk, reactive way.

**A couple of examples with and without mirroring:**

*Husband:* I'm quitting my job. I just can't stand working for those people.

*Wife A:* (understandably anxious) But how will

you support the family? You are overreacting. Is it really that bad to throw away all of those years with the company? How will you get hired elsewhere at a comparable salary?

*Wife B:* (also anxious, but putting the anxiety aside to mirror): So you want to quit your job? You can't stand those people you work with. It sounds like you had a hard day. Do you want to tell me more about it?

While the husband's statement could surely be anxiety-provoking, see how the mirroring shifted the flow of the conversation? The first version could have easily ended with frustration, even more anxiety, and possibly a fight. The second version, where the wife mirrored, would have resulted in stronger connection. Perhaps the husband would have cooled down and realized that after expressing his frustration, he really did not intend to quit. Maybe the wife would have understood why he should quit.

## Another example of a direct attack:

*Wife:* I can't believe you are home late again. Every single night you are at the office and you don't even bother calling.

*Husband A:* (feeling attacked) The last thing I need to hear after a hard day's work is your constant complaining. I told you I had a lot of work this week. Could you just give me a break?

*Husband B:* (feeling attacked, but deciding to mirror) You're upset that I am late and that I am at the office late every night and I don't call you to tell you when I am coming home. Is that right?

Instead of turning into a shouting match, the husband who mirrors holds on to his reactivity and defuses the conflict by giving his wife a voice.

While it requires a lot of discipline not to respond, it is worth the effort. It allows you to remain calm and not slip into reactivity. It gets you to feel safe enough to hear what the other is saying without taking it as a personal attack. Instead of every interchange penetrating your heart like a dagger, chipping away at your sense of well-being, you are holding up a mirror to reflect and deflect.

Mirroring is also beneficial for the one being mirrored. Whenever there is conflict, reactivity, or resistance in a relationship, it is a sign that somebody is feeling unsafe. Mirroring defuses the emotional charge from the other side and allows one to feel safe. Your spouse no longer needs to prove his or her point or protect himself or herself by being reactive. He or she feels heard.

# So When Do You Mirror?

Of course, you will want to mirror when your spouse is emotionally triggered, or when there is a difficult subject being discussed that might trigger you. You may also want to mirror anything your spouse tells you, even an appreciation she shares. In a tense relationship full of conflict, even the most benign comment can trigger a reaction. Mirroring helps avoid any potential misunderstandings or misinterpretations.

The general rule is: when in doubt, mirror. Regardless of the situation, you can't go wrong mirroring. (Of course, it needs to sound natural; otherwise, your spouse will think you are mimicking.)

## *An example:*

After a hard day of work and helping around the house, I needed to unwind. The kids were in bed and I needed to prepare for a singles group that would be arriving in 15 minutes. I walked into the kitchen and my wife starts asking me to help her do this or that. She asks me for a frying pan. I think to myself, Please stop asking me to do things. Can't you see that I need to get ready? Plus, I just spent the last hour helping to get dinner together, do the dishes, and putting the kids to bed. Instead of reacting out of frustration, I thought to myself, "Just mirror that back." That is what I did: "So you want me to get out that frying pan?" I wound up taking out the frying pan, and I did it in a way that helped me not resent it and not be reactive. Mirroring such a trivial thing helped prevent us from a needless blow-up. So again, you can't go wrong if you mirror.

The final thing to remember is that this is not a "trick" to use on your unknowing spouse. This is a way of being in your relationship, of allowing another to be heard and to train your brain to respond from a place of safety, not reactivity.

Your relationship will be much more enjoyable and the walls of resistance erected by you and your spouse will come crumbling down.

## But How Does Anything Actually Get "Fixed?"

I hope you have a clearer idea of the purpose of the dialogue and the wonders it can do for your relationship. A common concern, which you may also be feeling, is how this actually "solves" anything. Couples wonder how improving communication will actually get a spouse to change or stop undesirable behavior.

A common occurrence in conventional marriage counseling is that the therapist serves as a mediator, conducting negotiations for the warring parties; The husband will take out the garbage if his wife agrees to make dinner. While it appears both sides got what they wanted, they also may feel that they are being coerced by the therapist to do something they do not want to do. Making deals often leads to resentment and competition: "Look at how much I do around the house . . . you could at least do this for me." The relationship is no better and new problems will arise.

When I work with couples, I do not negotiate or attempt conflict resolution. I believe, and have seen on numerous occasions, that change occurs through dialogue. As I mentioned above, dialogue enables couples to have a stronger connection. Often the listener, or receiver, has so much compassion for a spouse's story that he or she wants to change. Sometimes, when the sender (the one talking) realizes that her frustration with her spouse is deeper than it appears on surface level, she no longer needs her spouse to change or be different.

In the case of the couple that dialogued about dry cleaning, the husband began to take more initiative when he realized there was more to his wife's story. The wife, upon realizing the depth of her story, became less reactive when her husband mentioned his to-do list.

In some cases, the sender may even take care of the situation by herself . Since she was heard, she is more relaxed and resourceful. An example of this occurred to a colleague of mine who was traveling on Thanksgiving weekend when he was dismayed to find that his connecting flight was cancelled. Passengers hounded the lady at the ticket counter, demanding she find them a flight. When my colleague approached her, he noticed her frazzled appearance. He acknowledged her by mirroring, validating, and empathizing her experience. He said, "Wow, I imagine you are having a rough time with all of these travelers. It makes a lot of sense that you would be exhausted and at your wits' end." By acknowledging her reality, he was able to give her the gift of feeling understood, which enabled her to be more resourceful and get him out on the next connecting flight. Was this a coincidence? No! When we are under stress we are ineffective. Emotional upset or frustration produces stress on the brain. It leaves us in an unresourceful state. When we can express our grievances and feel heard, we can remove the stress associated with those frustrations and be able to use our brain to the fullest, often thinking of solutions that would be otherwise obvious to someone not under stress.

Finally, as we have seen above, when there is connection, problems work themselves out because they are usually about more than the specific issues initially raised.

## Summary of Action Step IV

You acknowledge the other when you speak and when you listen. When you speak, keep the goal in mind. Why am I bringing this issue up? Do I intend to connect or do I want to dump? Is it a good time? If your goal is connection, make sure your spouse is ready to hear what you have to say. If it is not a good time, reschedule.

When you listen you can acknowledge the other by entering the world of the other, listening and understanding in the context of his or her reality. As we are naturally self-absorbed, we develop a sense of symbiosis, that my reality is "the reality." In a relationship, we experience the rude awakening that there are two realities, two truths, and our job is to break that symbiosis and experience the truth of the other.

We can break the symbiosis and enter the world of the other by listening to the other as opposed to responding from our own reactions. This other-focused listening helps us curb our own reactivity. It also helps us realize that our spouse's frustration is only 10% about the issue at hand, and 90% about something deeper. When we understand his/her story, it allows us to have more compassion for him/her.

The Imago Dialogue is a structured and safe process for taking your listening to the next level. It helps control reactivity and makes it possible to truly enter the world of the other, resulting in deep connection and relationship change. Problems are often fixed organically when we engage in this process. Those who have compassion for their spouse's underlying story often want to change on their own. We also become more resourceful when we feel heard and can often solve the problem on our own.

You have worked hard on creating safety in your relationship, yet there is one remaining ingredient to add to the mix — what I like to call love infusions. Love infusions are activities that promote positive energy in your relationship. Like a shot of adrenalin, they infuse your relationship with new vigor. Entering the world of the other and talking about serious issues can get a little heavy at times. Love infusions help lighten up the relationship and add fun. This is especially important, as, according to psychologist Dr. John Gottman's research, we must have a 5:1 ratio of posi-tive-to-negative interactions everyday, and those positive interactions are the key to predicting the success and longevity of a relationship.

# ACTION STEP V: LOVE INFUSIONS

## APPRECIATIONS

One of my favorite love infusions is appreciations. I can't overemphasize the importance of expressing appreciation for your spouse. When you are feeling resentful it may be hard to see the good in your spouse, yet it is precisely at that moment that you can make the shift from negativity to feelings of fondness. The more you express what you appreciate about your spouse, the better you will feel. In turn, your spouse's resentment will diminish, as he or she realizes that you appreciate him or her. It will also reinforce the positive behavior: "Wow, look at the re-sponse I received for taking out the garbage. I'll make sure I do it again." Thus, one appreciation can cause a build-up of positive energy in your relationship.

The best way to express an appreciation is if you have your spouse's full attention. Assuming you even think to thank your spouse for making your lunch, are you running out the door, yell-ing from another room, or calling on your cell phone? Making sure you have a real face-to-face moment to share your appreciation allows both parties to really be present with each other.

If you want to deepen your appreciation, share with your spouse the reason you appreci-ate him/her. This goes beyond a mere thank-you and expresses your thanks on an emotional level, which can touch your spouse's heart. Remember that when you are providing the reason for the appreciation, it must be purely positive. Back-handed compliments with negative implications do not express true appreciation and can be poisonous to a marriage. (Ex: "Thanks a lot for doing x,y,z, because you never do!") By focusing on the positive, couples increase positive energy and return to a good place in their relationship, to their original sense of connection.

For those on the receiving end, how would you typically respond if you were being thanked for making lunch? "No problem, it was nothing, my pleasure, you're welcome, sure...". Maybe you weren't even listening. When you hear an appreciation, try to really take in your spouse's kind words and to feel the positive sentiment that he or she is expressing. You may even want to initially mirror back the appreciation without responding at all. When you mirror what your spouse says you are compelled to listen and not interject, argue, or even belittle his/her own efforts. If a spouse is not able to receive the love that the partner is showing, he/she prevents the positive energy occasioned by such interactions and disregards this opportunity to build happiness.

Even something that is seemingly trivial or obvious should be articulated. Besides the aforementioned benefits of expressing gratitude, the benefits of articulating appreciations are twofold. By becoming more conscious, the one sharing the appreciation will experience increased feelings of gratitude towards his or her spouse, and the one on the receiving end will feel good that his or her actions were noticed. Feelings of resentment or being taken for granted start to dissipate, and the relationship quickly shifts.

Not only does this exercise infuse joy into relationships, it also motivates change. When one is constantly feeling appreciated, he/she will be motivated to continue those actions.

Try making time to share appreciations. Whether it is once a day or once a week, it will do wonders for your relationship.

## DATE NIGHT

Another essential love infusion is date night. With your busy schedule and possible disinterest in your relationship it might be extremely challenging to make time to go out with your spouse. Let me make a suggestion. . . plan time to have fun. Planning fun? How boring! While it may not sound so spontaneous, it may be the only way that you will ever get around to enjoying each other's company.

My wife and I have had a standing date night for the last two or three years. We found a babysitter who comes every Tuesday night to give us an opportunity to get out and spend time together. While this does not substitute daily interaction, which is necessary, it keeps the relationship in a positive space and also defuses a lot of potential conflict.

By making a set time, you are demonstrating with concrete action that you are committed to your relationship. Couples often have the best intentions to spend time with each other, but in their hectic lives, they don't always wind up making the time. Before we made our date night, my wife would nag me to go out. As I am more of a homebody, I presented an array of excuses on a regular basis. Although I wanted to spend time with her, my indifference sent her a message that I was not interested. Since I blocked out my Tuesday nights for the two of us, this issue disappeared. Once in a while something will come up and we need to cancel, but it rarely has a negative impact on our relationship because we know that we have made going out a priority in our relationship.

I have found this easy to generalize to almost anything significant in life. We all know the importance of exercise, yet why is it so hard for many of us to actually do it? My most successful periods of life, in terms of physical fitness, were when I had an appointment to work out. If you have a trainer expecting you or an exercise class you attend, you will show up. If you merely hope to get around to it, it is unlikely to happen.

For couples steeped in negativity, date night is crucial. It will help rekindle the flame and allow you to experience some of the fun times that made you fall in love with your spouse in the first place. This also provides hope for the relationship, reminding you of the many positive things that you still share together.

## Love Her

But what if you feel that you no longer love your spouse? What good will any of these love infusions do? Dr. Steven Covey tells the following story in *The Seven Habits of Highly Effective People*:

After a marriage seminar, a man approached Dr. Covey and told him that he no longer loved his wife. "I just don't love her anymore." Dr. Covey replied, "Then love her." The husband was a bit confused, "I told you, the feeling just isn't there anymore." Again, Dr. Covey replied, "Then love her." [3]

While you may feel that the fire has gone out of your relationship, if you increase your loving acts to your spouse, you will come to love her. This means doing caring behaviors, specific acts that are done unconditionally to make your spouse feel loved and cared for. Think about what your spouse enjoys and do it. Cook him his favorite dinner, buy her flowers. Not only will you generate love from your spouse, you will also begin to feel more love.

One common frustration that couples have is that they feel that they are giving to their spouse, yet they are still met with criticism that they are not doing enough. While there may be an element of negativity and inability to receive the gifts being offered, many times these couples are simply missing the mark.

We typically express our care for our spouse in the way we know best; the way that makes us feel cared for. If we feel cared for when people buy us presents then we will express our love for our spouse by buying them gifts.

While this may be well-intentioned, it may not be what your spouse wants or needs to feel cared for. Begin to think about what makes your spouse feel loved or cared for. You may even want to ask him or her, if appropriate. As you learn more about what makes him or her feel loved, you may notice that it is very different than what you need. As you begin to hit the mark, you will see that the resentment that you may have been met with previously will dissipate and your efforts will be received in a positive manner that will serve to increase the love in your relationship.

One more point, which applies both to date night and love infusions: There are many cute books with ideas for how to be more romantic or show love for your spouse. These books can be helpful in providing ideas, especially for those who are not necessarily so fun or spontaneous. It is important to note that such recommendations do not necessarily mean that your spouse will react as positively as you hope.

Above all, know your spouse. If you don't want to ask them, try to remember what they used to like to do when you first dated. What activities did they enjoy? What made them excited? Use recommendations from books and friends as a springboard to start thinking about what your spouse may like.

Love infusions are necessary to increase the positive energy in any relationship. A little light can push away a lot of darkness, so do not underestimate the powers of the aforementioned activities or any other positive or fun interaction you can have with your spouse. Even if you have not mastered Action Steps I-IV, infusing love in your marriage can help bring you to a relationship state where you will be able to better implement the first four Action Steps. If you are in crisis, you may feel like you are forcing yourself, but eventually you will see how vital love infusions are to your relationship and enjoy them!

## SUMMARY OF ACTION STEP V

Love infusions bring positive energy into your relationship. They are necessary in any relationship, especially to combat any potential negativity.

Appreciations are a way of expressing gratitude to our spouse. Not only do they reinforce positive behavior, they decrease resentment, and lead to more positive energy in the relationship. They also allow the recipient to truly feel appreciated.

By scheduling a weekly date night on your calendar, you are showing commitment to your relationship with real action. Date night is an opportunity for you to have fun with each other and rekindle the flame that you once experienced.

Even when we do not have positive feelings for our spouse it is important to engage in actions that demonstrate our care and love. When we act with love, we not only increase our spouse's feelings of love for us, we begin to develop more feelings of love for our spouse.

# 5

## The

## CONCLUSION: YOU'VE MADE IT!

## CONCLUSION

Congratulations! You are now one step closer to transforming your marriage from destruction to delight. Let's review the 5 Action Steps you have taken:

## ACTION STEP I - COMMIT

You stopped looking elsewhere and started looking again to your spouse for your relationship needs. You recommitted to your marriage, realizing that is not expendable like a computer.

And you stopped thinking that marrying someone else would make things better, becoming
aware that the issues in your relationship are really vehicles for growth and healing.

## ACTION STEP II - SEAL YOUR EXITS

You created your safe relationship room,
shutting off any exits you may have taken from
your relationship. You also became aware of any
external influences on your relationship that
may have been sabotaging your marriage.

## ACTION STEP III- DETOX YOUR MARRIAGE

You began eliminating all negativity,
blame, and shame from your relationship. You
learned how your frustrations were really requests and that if you could ask for what you

wanted in a safe way, your spouse would be much more receptive.

## Action Step IV - Acknowledge the "Other"

You learned how to keep the goal in mind when sharing or listening, by making sure it was a good time to talk. You also learned a new way to listen by entering the world of the other, thereby controlling your own reactivity and allowing your spouse to be heard.

## Action Step V - Love Infusions

You began to inject positive energy into your relationship with appreciations, a weekly date night, and caring behaviors meant to reawaken love for your spouse.

You are now at the end of this book but at the beginning  of your relationship journey. As you have learned, it takes action, but the positive results are well worth the effort. Wishing you much success and a lifetime of happiness together!

If you have any questions about what you've just read, I encourage you to visit:

**www.TheMarriageRestorationProject.com**

# THE 5 STEP ACTION PLAN
## FULL PROGRAM

A multisensory experience consisting of five audio CDs, a DVD, and a workbook, the Full Program brings the material alive in an easy to follow and digestible format. From communication failures to anger to affairs, this program addresses the gamut of pain that couples all over are experiencing in a private, sensitive, and economical way.

To learn more about this program, please visit:

**www.TheMarriageRestorationProject.com**

## The 2-day Marriage Restoration Intensive

The 2-Day Intensive is the ultimate solution for those on the brink of divorce who wish to make a last-ditch effort to save their marriage. After two full days in private session working on your relationship, you will say goodbye to old destructive patterns, discover new tools that will get you through the rough patches time and time again, and fall back in love. The 2-Day Marriage Restoration Intensive provides the hope that your relationship really can be better.

To learn more about this program, please visit:

**www.TheMarriageRestorationProject.com**

# ACKNOWLEDGMENTS

I would like to acknowledge the work

of Drs. Harville Hendrix and Helen LaKelly Hunt who

developed Imago Relationship Therapy. All of the

Imago ideas, concepts, and techniques found in this

book are based on their work.